The Alchemist's Oracle

ELIXIRS FOR PERSONAL
GROWTH & WELLBEING

Zoe Sadler

**The Alchemist's Oracle:
Elixirs for Personal Growth & Wellbeing**
Copyright © 2025 Zoe Sadler

All rights reserved. Other than for personal use, no part of these cards or this book may be reproduced in any way, in whole or part, without the written consent of the copyright holder or publisher. All references to alchemy and the mixing of substances and potions in this card deck and guidebook are intended to be metaphorical only. No potions or substances mentioned are intended for actual consumption. These cards are intended for spiritual and emotional guidance. The content is not intended to replace medical assistance or treatment. The views and opinions expressed by the author, both within and outside of this publication, do not necessarily reflect the views of the publisher.

Published by Blue Angel Publishing®
10 Trafford Court, Wheelers Hill
Victoria, Australia 3150

info@blueangelpublishing.com
www.blueangelpublishing.com

Edited by Peter Loupelis and Cherise Asmah
Designed by Gemma Christensen and Sunshine Connelly

Blue Angel is a registered trademark of Blue Angel Gallery Pty Ltd.

ISBN: 978-1-922574-25-1

Table of Contents

PRIMA MATERIA

Unveiling the Arcanum	8
Using the Arcanum Divinora	23

ARCANUM MATERIA

A Wish	36
Beetle Juice	38
Befuddlement	41
Bird Song	44
Blood of the Undead	46
Bone Dust	49
Crows' Feet	51
Dandelion Root	54
Dead Sea Salt	57
Deadly Nightshade	60
Digitalis	63
Dragon's Breath	66
Dreamcatcher	69
Elixir of Life	72
Fairy Liquid	74
Good Fortune	77
Graveyard Dust	80
Lightning Bolt	83
Lily of the Valley	86
Liquid Moonlight	89
Love Potion	91

Mandrake Root	94
Mermaid's Song	97
Mermaid's Tears	100
Night Owl Potion	103
Octopus Ink	105
Phoenix Fire	107
Poison	110
Poison Ivy	113
Pumpkin Juice	116
Rainbow Dust	118
Rats' Blood	121
Revive	124
Seahorse Scales	127
Shroomka	130
Sleeping Draught	133
Snake Venom	136
Spider Venom	139
Spirit	142
Stardust	144
Storm in a Bottle	147
Sunbeams	150
Tincture of Toad	153
Truth Serum	156
Unicorn Horn Dust	159
Valerian	162
Wolfsbane	164
Wormwood	167
About the Creator	170

*T*AKE *it from the oracle,*

And consider it forbade.

This deck is purely metaphorical,

And no potion is to be consumed or made!

(In other words, do not attempt to make or consume these potions.
This deck is all metaphorical fun!)

Alchemy

[noun] A form of chemistry studied in the Middle Ages that involved trying to discover how to change ordinary metals into gold.

[literary] A mysterious power or magic that can change things.

Oxford Learners Dictionary

Prima Materia

Unveiling the Arcanum

Alchemy is an ancient art shrouded in magic and mystery. Its secrets passed down through generations. Over the years, alchemists have honed their craft, seeking ways to turn lead into gold or concoct the elusive Elixir of Life. Alchemy within the purpose of this deck is represented as a spiritual practice, the intention being to transform yourself and live an enriched life, filled with meaning and purpose. The potions and ingredients are metaphors for different parts of our being and things we experience in life.

MY ARTISANAL JOURNEY

I've always wanted to transform the everyday and mundane into something extraordinary and fantastical. My entire life has not just been a creative journey but a spiritual one. Early on, I recognised that I was not only creative by nature, but also more sensitive than others — a 'highly sensitive person' (HSP). I've always been in tune with emotions, and intuitive and empathetic toward others. Discovering alchemy began a journey of self-discovery to understand and connect more deeply with myself, and find the contentment and peace we all wish to have in our lives.

I love nature and the outdoors, whether it's having a reviving swim in the sea or just feeling at peace under a tree — it's my calm centre. I also have a keen interest in the medicinal use of plants and herbs. I enjoy foraging for plants to add to skincare remedies, to add to food, or to make my own inks and paints. It's my form of making potions — alchemy. I have endlessly researched and studied the symbology of plants and animals and enjoy fairy tale stories, myths, and legends; and of course, alchemy and the history of witches. All this has led me to compile everything I've learnt and experienced to produce *The Alchemist's Oracle*.

THE ALCHEMICAL OPUS

This deck is here to help inspire you and help you on a journey toward self-love and better emotional wellbeing by exploring your inner wisdom; a way for you to help discover yourself and your true path. This deck is your spirit guide on this journey. This is *your* alchemical process to change your life. Just as alchemy is a way to transform lead into gold, consider this deck a pathway toward your personal transformation. It will enrich your life and add meaning and purpose.

Historically, there are seven stages to the alchemical process (to turn lead into gold), or as we will call it, our alchemical or spiritual journey:

1. **Calcination** — This is the catalyst. A fire has been lit inside you and sparked you into action. This is the time to pick up your deck and begin your alchemical journey to find yourself.

2. **Dissolution** — The time to break it all apart. You might have been feeling a little broken. This is the time to look inside yourself and find all those individual pieces. Shuffle the cards and focus on those pieces.

3. **Separation** — Separate all those parts out within yourself. Delve deep and look at all

those pieces of yourself to be able to begin your transformation of self. Pick a card or cards.

4. **Conjunction** — Rebuild those broken pieces. Repairing your unconscious self to become more aware. Turn over the card(s) and let them guide and inspire you.

5. **Fermentation** — The time to contemplate and mull things over. The real transformation—to understand yourself better—has begun. Read the meanings behind the cards and remember they are open to your interpretation — they are here to guide you or give you a feeling. Not to tell you what to do. Use your intuition. Only you will really know the best path forward.

6. **Distillation** — Purify your thoughts and let them settle over you and bring you peace. A good time to meditate, allowing your mind to find serenity and calm.

7. **Coagulation** — Bringing you back to the whole, making you solid and steady again. The transformation is complete, and you have let the cards guide you and transform you into something more stable. A better version of you that already existed. You have just recognised it. You are strong and whole. A sparkly human, enriched and full of the vitality of life. You are truly living!

... FIRE BURN AND CAULDRON BUBBLE ...

Each oracle card is based upon a magic potion …

A magic potion is quite simply a drink with magical properties. Generally, a potion will either have a magical power, be a poison, medicine, tonic, or remedy to cure an illness or quite simply perk you up a bit!

All the potions in this deck are transformative, which is how they apply to alchemy. And of course, they have been concocted and brewed by your very own inky alchemist. These potions all have a spiritual meaning to transform and enrich your life and help you on your alchemical journey.

By choosing a card, you are metaphorically uncorking a magic potion to drink in the meaning of what the card contains. You can metaphorically chug the whole lot, or just take a few drops, depending on how you feel or how much you think the card relates to you at a given time — it's your choice. There may even be the odd occasion where you feel that a card isn't right for you at this time. That's okay too. Use your intuition and your magic potions wisely.

AS ABOVE, SO BELOW

Each card or magic potion is associated with a different alchemical symbol or occasionally more than one. This is after all an alchemy deck and adds to the overall sense or interpretation you might get from the cards.

It may be as simple as the symbol to represent one of the four elements; *earth*, *air*, *fire*, or *water*. These are fairly self-explanatory when you consider them in context to the potion shown on the card. They may also correspond with alchemical substances such as *salt,* which represents purity and the body, or *sulphur* which represents the soul. Some planetary metals are included in the deck because of their association with their planets but also different parts of the human body, such as *gold* (often referred to as the Sun) which points to the heart, or *iron,* which corresponds with the planet Mars and is associated with blood. See the following list for an overview of the alchemical symbols used in this deck and what meaning they bring to the cards.

Please note: Some artistic license has been used in the depiction of these symbols.

The Philosopher's Stone

In alchemy, this is typically known as the substance to transform base metals like lead or mercury into gold, and used to create the Elixir of Life. Therefore, the alchemical symbol in a spiritual sense represents transformation as well as the renewal or revival of spirit. It can also indicate a path or journey to success.

 # Air

Air represents life. It is an uplifting symbol. Breathing new life and inspiration to the everyday. An uplifted sense of spirit.

EARTH

Earth represents grounding energy, stability, and stillness. As well as untapped potential and growth.

FIRE

This is the most volatile of the four basic elements. It represents fiery emotions such as passion, love, and even hate.

WATER

This basic element represents change and in terms of this deck often indicates changing tides or more simply put, the highs and lows of life. It can signify changing fortunes, feminine energy, powerful forces, and vitality.

Phosphorus

Phosphorus in this deck represents an additional basic element of *spirit* so refers to spiritual practices and enlightenment.

Mercury

Mercury, also known as 'quicksilver', represents the mind. It signifies the shift between life and death, symbolising rebirth, renewal, and the transition between these states. It embodies balance. Mercury (the Greek god Hermes) was the Roman messenger to the gods, thus representing communication. Additionally, it is associated with the lungs.

Salt

This is a pure substance, so it represents purification and good intentions as well as protection. Symbolises the body.

Sulphur

Also known as 'brimstone', so most often linked with the element of fire and therefore the devil. It also symbolises the soul, and the substance can act as a soul cleanser, creating a sense of clarity and peace. Protection against negative energy.

Gold

In simple terms, *gold* represents the Sun and sunlight. So symbolises positivity, joy, and abundance. It can also represent magnetic personalities. Represents the heart.

Copper

Represents the planet Venus so indicates love, relationships, and connection. Associated with the kidneys.

Silver

Silver represents the night and the Moon. It also symbolises intuition and contemplation. It is often seen alongside the water element or where there is a strong feminine energy present. Also associated with the brain.

Iron

Represents strength and fortitude. A resilient nature, and thus symbolises blood.

Antimony

Represents the animalistic side of human nature and is traditionally represented by the wolf.

Diamond

Represents the female spirit or feminine energy.

Sand of Time

Represents transformation and is a well-known catlyst for change. So can symbolise the end of something and the beginning of a new phase.

Purity

Represents purity.

Ashes

The end of something and new beginnings, like a phoenix rising from the ashes.

Pentagram

Symbolises creativity and connection. All the basic elements in harmony with one another.

Other Symbols

The cards contain other hidden symbols and meanings. Of course, the magic potion on each card has the most significant relevance to its meaning, backed up by its corresponding alchemical symbol. For instance, some cards contain plants and their herbal uses or are derived from ancient folklore and magic or spiritual practices. The appearance of magical creatures is also a strong theme throughout the cards. All this and more has been channelled into each card to provide meaning and give you inspiration and positivity which you can use in everyday life.

Creatures you might encounter include dragons, fairies, mermaids, toads, phoenixes, unicorns, and many more. Botanicals such as lavender, dandelion, and valerian, as well as their more poisonous counterparts such as ivy, deadly nightshade (Belladonna), and foxglove (Digitalis) also appear. For example, lavender promotes sleep and rest and is therefore paired with the alchemical symbol for *silver/Moon*, indicating that you may need more rest or are having trouble sleeping. Ivy can be interpreted in two ways as it can be suffocating or supportive depending on what you are asking the cards or how you feel at the time. Dragons—representing transformation amongst other secondary meanings like strength and power—are most often paired with the element of *fire*. A simple goldfish can mean good fortune and abundance and be paired with the *gold/Sun* symbol.

You will also find the inclusion of smaller symbols such as feathers, skulls, or moons. It is even worth looking at the shapes of the bottles or their stoppers, as they too could have a meaning or speak to you as the reader of the cards. They might resonate with you or add another secret meaning to the card. Don't forget to look at both the card backgrounds and each individual illustration when you conduct a reading.

Each card's explanation will refer to these hidden meanings in some form or other. Some themes will recur throughout the deck and others may just be one-offs.

THROUGH A SHADOW DARKLY...

The cards have an equal mix of black and white backgrounds. For example, cards that emphasise the Sun or light will generally have a white background and those that represent (let's say) a creature of the night or the Moon will have a dark one. However, don't be fooled, as this is not always the case. All the cards have a lighter meaning and a shadow side no matter which background they may have.

For instance, you would probably expect the *Fairy Liquid* card to have a white background, but the fairy here is depicted as a light in the dark, so she is shown in white, shining brightly in the darkness.

The cards are also not intended to have a reverse meaning. Suppose you draw a card upside down. In that case, it doesn't necessarily point to a negative connotation as traditionally seen in some tarot readings. It doesn't matter which way up you draw a card. It is for you to interpret the card's meaning in relation to how you feel or where you are in your particular alchemical or spiritual journey.

Similar to tarot, some of the cards may at first glance appear to have a darker interpretation, but more often indicate the end of something, the beginning of a new phase in your life, or stepping out of darkness and into the light — such as the cards *Graveyard Dust* or *Poison*. No card has negative connotations; instead, they encourage you to consider all aspects of your life and how you approach and fill your days with positivity and joy. Like alchemy, the cards represent transformation and ways to live an enriching and fulfilling life.

Using the Arcanum Divinora

CONJURING THE ARCANUM: PREPARING YOUR DECK

There are no set rules to how you use your deck; they are yours to use as you see fit. Your cards will work better for you when used instinctively. There are a couple of different interpretations for each card (for all but *A Wish*). Sometimes, one meaning may be more relevant to you than another. You may also simply need the wisdom of the affirmation. Trust your intuition, and you'll get the medicine you need. Here are a few tips to get you started.

First of all, you will want to cleanse or clear your deck. Your cards are sensitive to different energies, absorbing energy from others who have been in contact with your deck. To make them truly yours, you want them to respond to your own energies.

- ◇ Place them out under the full moon overnight, one of the most powerful ways to refresh your cards.
- ◇ Burn sage, a smudge stick, or any other (ethically sourced) sacramental incense and pass the cards through the smoke.
- ◇ Visualise the energies surrounding your cards, and focus on clearing the space around them. As this is a potion-themed deck, perhaps you could visualise a cleansing potion that you sprinkle or spritz around your cards. Alternatively, spritz some of your own favourite scent around them to help you connect with them deeply.

Once you have cleansed and feel you have connected with your cards, it is a good idea to familiarise yourself with the deck before a first reading.

Don't forget to give your cards a good shuffle before their first use. Think of it like swirling a potion or cauldron to mix all the ingredients. The best way to do this is to spread them face down on a flat surface in front of you and swirl the cards around, mixing them up. Intuitively you will know when they are ready. You are now prepared for your first reading and to uncork your first potion.

ENGAGING THE DIVINORA

Choose a quiet space to conduct a reading. Switch off all technology and distractions. You can also cleanse your space to clear away negative energies. If you like to connect with nature, why not take your deck outside onto the grass, or choose a favourite relaxing spot or somewhere you feel inspired.

The easiest way to use your cards is simply to hold the deck in your hands. Give them a little shuffle and settle on a thought or feeling — perhaps you have a question you want to direct at the deck. Focus on your thought or question while you shuffle, sensing how your thoughts and feelings are infusing the cards in your hands. As before, visualise the swirling and mixing of a potion if that helps you connect with your cards.

When you are ready, pick a single card from the deck. You can do this by:

- ◊ Spreading the cards out face down in front of you
- ◊ Placing the cards in front of you one by one until you find one you are most drawn to
- ◊ Cutting the deck and choosing either the bottom card of the first pile, or the top card of the second pile

Occasionally a card might fall out of the deck, peek out, or even fly out as you shuffle. Pay particular attention to these cards — the deck might be trying to tell you something. You can either focus on this card alone, or place it alongside an already picked card. It might add further clarity to the question or intention you are projecting onto the deck. Never ignore a spilt potion — wipe it up and address it!

Another typical spread is the three-card spread, where the first card represents your past, the middle your present and the third your future.

However, if you wish to undertake a more complex reading (or, let's say, mix a more complicated potion) you might like to try one of these:

THE ELEMENTAL SPREAD

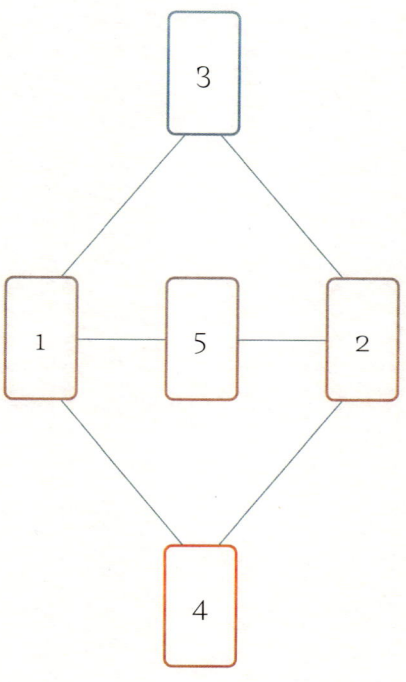

THE ELEMENTAL SPREAD

This is the perfect spread to take outside and into nature, and it's helpful when you are looking for some inspiration (a tonic) or facing a problem you require a remedy for. The elements are important and should always be considered whenever you brew or concoct a potion. For instance, the weather can have a bearing on a concoction or reading as it can affect the mood of the alchemist or reader; stormy, and the outcome or interpretation might be more volatile; rain might indicate a more changeable outcome; and on a sunny or golden day, doesn't everything seem more positive? They can affect the outcome or make it more or less potent.

Please note that the lines intersecting the cards within this spread have a bearing on the reading and how you interpret the cards. For instance, as the *Spirit* card (Card Five) is positioned at the centre of the spread, it serves as the focal point that links to all the other cards, making it the determining factor for the overall meaning. In this arrangement, each of the surrounding cards influences its ultimate interpretation. Cards One, Five, and Two have a close connection running through them. Note the shapes made from the lines give us the alchemical symbols for fire and water, showing their placement within the spread is also relevant, with Card Five connecting the surrounding four elements.

You can refer to the alchemical guide to remind yourself of the symbols, but using your own intuition is just as important when conducting a reading and translating the meanings. Trust in your intuition and let the elements be your guide.

Card One: Earth — What grounds you?

Card Two: Air — What inspires or lifts you?

Card Three: Fire — What challenges you?

Card Four: Water — What must you change or learn from?

Card Five: Spirit — The Outcome

THE ALCHEMICAL JOURNEY SPREAD

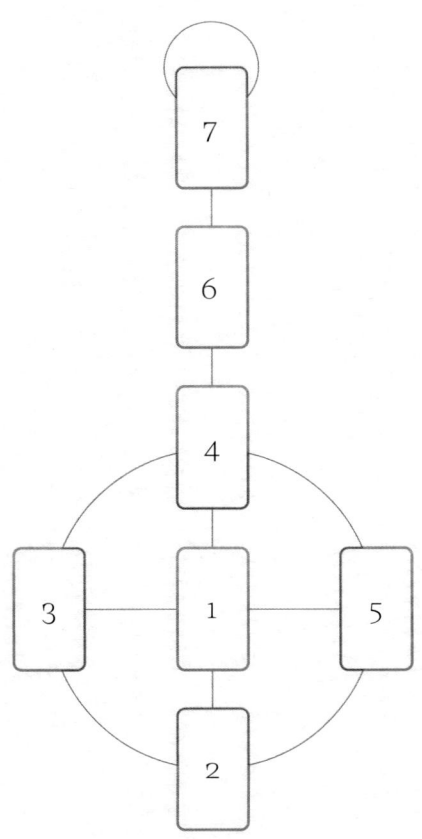

THE ALCHEMICAL JOURNEY SPREAD

If you are looking for something a little more in-depth, this spread is ideal if you are on the start of a new path, journey, or feeling a bit stuck in life and not sure what is next for you. It is designed to provide clarity or unlock something within you. This spread is about your spiritual journey. Like the alchemical process of turning lead into gold and creating the Elixir of Life, this spread describes transformation.

Please note, the lines intersecting the cards within this spread also have a bearing on the reading and how you interpret the cards.

For instance, Card One represents yourself as you are now, so relates to all the other cards as it is central to the spread.

Cards Three, One, and Five represent your past, present, and future respectively.

Cards One to Five can be read separately and in conjunction with one another as a whole. The circle they are contained within can also represent the symbol for salt (the body of the spread) and also gold (the heart of the spread). Depending on the context, you may be drawn to one symbol or the other, and it may have a bearing on the overall interpretation of the spread. You can use your intuition here.

Cards Four to Seven have a close relationship to one another and are a culmination of the final outcome (Card Seven). Note the overall shape of this spread represents a stoppered potion, so Cards Four to Seven can be interpreted metaphorically as the final concoction brewed from the potion, Cards One to Five.

How you deal with (or drink in) the final outcome is up to you. You might want to keep a stopper on it, tentatively remove the stopper, or it might just pop out and give you your eureka moment. It is your choice and how you feel at the time …

Card One: Calcination — Where you are now. What sets your soul on fire?

Card Two: Dissolution — What is affecting you or breaking you? What is your challenge?

Card Three: Separation — What hinders you? What is on your mind?

Card Four: Conjunction — What will help you or inspire you?

Card Five: Fermentation — What is the way forward? What are you learning?

Card Six: Distillation — What do you need to let go of?

Card Seven: Coagulation — Final outcome

Remember, you are the alchemist of your own life. The cards are here to guide you — but ultimately it is your interpretation and what you glean from the process that determine how this deck will work for you. Use these alchemical ingredients wisely and with lively intent.

THE RADIANT PROMISE

So, with a pinch of gold dust, a dash of foresight, and a generous measure of wit and charm you are left to use your deck to bring positivity and light into your days on this magical earth. Use the oracle cards intuitively to interpret and reflect upon your life. Let these magical potions and alchemical ingredients uplift and guide you, transforming your leaden life into gold!

ARCANUM MATERIA

A Wish

(AIR)

Manifest your dreams with faith and positivity by releasing a star-filled potion and focusing on your deepest desires.

AFFIRMATION

I am strong and powerful enough to grant my own wishes. My deepest desires and dreams can and will come true.

Close your eyes and wish upon a star.

Set your intentions. Concentrate on your greatest wish or desire. See it in your mind's eye and watch it materialise and come to fruition. You can manifest your deepest desires if only you believe. You don't need a fairy godmother to grant your wishes, trust instead in your inner and most powerful self. Be safe knowing that all your dreams can come true with a little bit of faith and positivity.

*A lone star twinkles shyly in a teeny tiny bottle.
But once released into the air it really shines.
The wish contained in this light-filled and sparkly
potion will grant your deepest desire or biggest wish.
Remember, a star symbolises positivity and renewal
and can act as a beacon. Release this potion into the
air around you and let it shine out and guide you.
Don't forget to recite your wish. It is your mantra for
today. Or simply recite the affirmation at the end
of this meaning.*

Beetle Juice

(GOLD)

Unleash your inner radiance and overcome doubts to embrace your shining destiny.

AFFIRMATION

I am strong and capable. I am an independent spirit with all I need to fulfil my destiny. I am the jewel that twinkles and sparkles in my own life.

You are on the right path and in charge of your own destiny. You are the jewel of your own life and have the ability to shine and draw good things to you. Spread your light and radiate it to others by complimenting a friend or smiling and acknowledging a passerby. It will bring good fortune to you and make you feel good about yourself.

Get up early and embrace the sunshine. Let it empower you. It will recharge you and give you more time to appreciate little everyday things, such as the feel of the sun's rays on your skin or the sweet smell of blossom on a morning walk. A smile and a little bit of positivity can open both your inner and outer world up to more possibilities and shiny new experiences, leading you to bigger and better things and a fresh new zest for life.

There may be an irritation or a nagging feeling you can't let go of. Don't let these feelings hold you back. You are more than capable of protecting and armouring yourself with whatever you need to overcome these doubts or fears and sparkle. Perhaps a friend is surrounding themselves in negativity and dragging you down with their pessimistic views. It might be time to gently intervene and let them know you are worried about them. Imagine yourself as a beacon or guiding light, radiating postivity over yourself and others.

If worst comes to worst, remember it's okay to see a little less of them to protect yourself. Although, perhaps still a good idea to check in with them from time to time to make sure they are okay. They will appreciate the thought, and it will make you feel better too.

Perhaps you are suffering from imposter syndrome at work. Be kinder to yourself and acknowledge all the hard work you have done to get to where you are now. You deserve it and are worthy of that future promotion or praise at work. You are a shiny and talented human that deserves the recognition and one who helps friends in need. But remember, you cannot help anyone without looking after yourself first.

A rare potion discovered in the lost tomb of an
Egyptian goddess. Just like Nefertiti, this potion allows
the bearer to shine like the Sun and glitter like gold.
The beetle represents the jewel-like qualities you possess
and the strength you already have within you.
Down this potion in one and let the effects radiate
from your centre and outwards into your life.

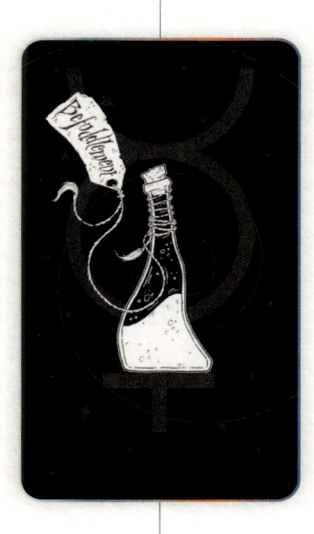

Befuddlement

(MERCURY)

Navigate confusion with caution, find clarity within, and seek support from trusted friends.

AFFIRMATION

I have organised my mind and I am ready to face any challenges or confusing situations that come my way.

It has been a confusing time, but the fog is lifting, giving you some clarity for the first time in a while. Take full advantage of this period of lucidity and get yourself organised. Write a list or keep a journal to keep things in check. Things will probably spiral and become crazy and confusing again, but you'll be well-equipped to handle all that life throws at you. Stress can cloud your judgement and throw you off balance, causing further befuddlement, so make time to manage it.

If the confusion just isn't lifting, take some time out. It is too easy to overthink and wind yourself up over nothing. Shut off the things that overwhelm you like digital devices and get away from the things that are causing you confusion. If it's work or a relationship, take yourself off for an hour or two. Go for a walk, read a book, or take a bath and go to bed early. Whatever is bothering you is probably not nearly as bad as you think and can probably be easily resolved. You could always talk things through with a friend. They might provide you with some clarity over a situation.

By confronting all that is throwing you off balance and addressing all that bewitches you, your mind will become clearer. Bringing you the energy for what matters and less regard for what doesn't.

You'll be infinitely more productive, giving you more freetime for play and fun times. Throwing off any lethargy and making you feel truly alive!

---

*A curious little potion. It may appear innocent and benign but as you watch the shifting and viscous liquid you feel more and more and more befuddled. Even the crudely made bottle appears to shift and warp of its own accord. Stare at it long enough and your thoughts may never become clear again. Use it wisely and sparingly. A few drops at a time to clear your mind. Too much and you might go a little doolally. Noting that **mercury** represents the mind, it was most likely concocted by a very long-lived alchemist with prolonged exposure to this element.*

Bird Song

(GOLD)

You are feeling uplifted and optimistic for the future. Your heart is brimming full of hopes and dreams.

AFFIRMATION

I sing to the beat of my own heart and therefore will shine brightly and bring beautiful things into my life. I am breaking out of the confines of my cage.

Bird Song fills your heart and mind; you might just find yourself humming happily away to yourself or singing in the shower. You are breaking free from the confines of your cage. Embrace this period of optimism and use it to work through any last negative thought patterns that hold you back. Now is the time to sing your little heart out and attract wonderful things into your life. This is an excellent time to travel or to embrace a new experience.

Don't become indifferent to what is happening around you just because life is good, it could mean you fall off your perch. Embracing your creativity or making time for something you love is the perfect way to make your heart sing. It can have a huge impact on your overall wellbeing and approach to life. It might even cause that cage door to fling open, giving you the room you really need to take off and fly, launch you onto a new trajectory, or fulfil a new career path. Remember, just like a bird's song you are unique and have your own voice.

A renowned alchemist with a penchant for ornithology discovered how to harness the power of birdsong. Nightingales symbolise joy and hope; this essence has been captured in this pretty little bird's song. Pop the cork to release your inner joy.

Blood of the Undead

Embrace transitions, follow your intuition, and guard against draining influences on your path to new beginnings.

AFFIRMATION

I am ready to embrace my soul purpose and project my intentions into something new and positive. I feel reborn.

A time of transition and new beginnings. You are ready to let go of the old to make room for the new. Leave the darkness behind and embrace the light and any new pathways that may present themselves to you. Soar high and enjoy the transcendent feeling the light brings but remember not to get too engrossed in all of this. You still need to stay grounded to avoid losing yourself in the rush. Let your intuition guide you. Perhaps you are in the throes of a new relationship and riding high on the excitement of being with a new partner. Or are thrilled to have been offered a high-flying new job. However, as good as things are right now, it may mean you have to make a few unforeseen sacrifices as you go. It's important to stay grounded in these situations so you don't land back down to earth with a bump after an initial take off.

To avoid getting too carried away, try this simple grounding exercise. Take off your shoes and socks and place your feet firmly on the ground. A natural surface is best. Close your eyes and concentrate on your breath.

Take deep, calming breaths as you connect with the ground beneath your feet. Even better, if it is warm and sunny outside, plant your feet on the grass and take a slow, meandering walk. Feel your breath become steadier and deeper and concentrate on the sensation of the soft grass caressing your feet as you walk. You can now enjoy the feel-good sensation of your surroundings without getting too carried away. You know in your heart you are moving along in the right direction, but it is wise to slow things down and go at a more sustainable pace.

Be aware of energy vampires on your travels from the dark into the light. Don't let other people's energy suck the life out of you and keep you from your soul purpose. Be mindful of who you give your time to; they may have a dark side they are trying to hide from you. You are very perceptive and can see what many others cannot. Trust your instincts and all will be fine.

Collected from vampire bats in the far corners of Romania by experienced vampire hunters, this potion is deadly in the wrong hands. You'll need an iron grip and superior strength to uncork this bottle. Bats represent transition, change and shadows.

Bone Dust

(IRON)

Revitalise your weary spirit, embrace new experiences, and rediscover the vibrancy within.

AFFIRMATION

I live life to the fullest and don't let the past drag me down. I look to bright new things so I can thrive.

You may be feeling downtrodden and tired of life, weary to the bone and physically exhausted. Don't let yourself feel defeated and downright dusty. Brush yourself off and face your problem areas head-on. Sitting and waiting for opportunities to unfold around you only leads to festering in negativity, letting time slip away. Grab life by the horns, and breathe in that new lease of energy!

Bored with your current routine, it's time to start a new hobby or do something active like go for a walk in nature. Feel more grounded by walking barefoot in the sand or swimming in the wild. It will give you a reinvigorated perspective and the zeal you lack. Fresh new soil or seeing things from a different point of view can help you grow. Nurture and feed your withered soul until you are once again the bright, beautiful, vibrant being you know you are.

*A dusty old bottle hides in the corner of a room, right at the back of a shelf filled with bone remnants and trinkets. The sharp tang of **iron** taints the air. Blowing off the dust, a sinister-looking skull stares back at you, goading you into opening the bottle and releasing the festering bone dust inside.*

Crows' Feet

Embrace transformation, trust your intelligence, and beware of deceptive influences.

AFFIRMATION

I am intelligent and clever and can adapt to any situation. I have the power and insight to transform my life.

You have it within yourself to transform your life.
Like the crow you are intelligent, clever, and insightful.
Use that ability to look inside yourself and find what
you might have lost or is missing from your life. You can
adapt to any situation; you have the power to make your
life fulfilling if you use what you have to your advantage.
To help you see things more clearly, try this visualisation:

> Concentrate on breathing in and out, slowly and
> deeply. On your next breath out, visualise yourself
> uncorking the stopper on your potion to release the
> contents. As you breathe, inhale the potion's essence.
> Imagine the vapour entwining itself around your
> senses, taking the form of a crow weaving itself
> around you, its wings fluttering and gently guiding
> you. You merge and transform with the crow, gliding
> and soaring off into the sky. You are carefree and take
> in the bird's eye view of your life as it is before you.

The bird helps you in the direction you need to go.
Is there something bothering you or getting in your way?
Is your perception of what you want your reality?
Look deep inside yourself, and ask if you are feeling
fulfilled. Is there something you can see yourself doing
which you are not doing currently? What do you want?
Let the bird play and your imagination with it. Visualise
doing the one thing you really want from life — where
does it lead you? If it appears challenging at first,

remember *you* are that bird and *you* have the power to transform your life into whatever you want. The bird has everything it needs to challenge those on its path and face down its foes, and so do you. You can soar high and free just like the crow. You know in your heart what it is you need to do — you just need to turn the realisation into reality.

A little bit of mischief now and then is fine, but remember, crows are known to have a wicked and devious side. They can be tricksters! So, keep a beady eye out for those who may deceive or try to manipulate you. Bad fortune will fall on those who do ill to others.

A lone crow hops into view. Quick-witted and mischievous, the crow appears to challenge you to face what is coming. Are you ready to uncork the bottle and face your challenges head-on? The crow symbolises transformation and change — so you pull out the stopper ...

Dandelion Root

(GOLD)

*Embrace hope, let worries fade,
and seize the joy of each day.*

AFFIRMATION

I live for today spreading sunshine, hope,
and optimism to others wherever I go.
Life is good.

The yellow petals of this golden-headed flower represent the Sun shining down on you and all the good in your life. As the seeds are carried into the air, they also carry your hopes and dreams and wishes. Spreading them far and wide brings new beginnings and a prosperous time to fruition.

If you are feeling blocked and just cannot see the good from the bad, try this simple exercise. Tear up some slips of paper. On each one, write down something positive in your life. You might even want to add in a hope for the future or a dream that you have. Take each slip of paper in turn, read each one aloud, and then gently blow upon it. Visualise the phrase you have written down being dispersed into the ether just like a dandelion seed.
Or even better, take a sunny walk and pick a dandelion, blowing on the seeds while sending your intention out into the world. You will release your joy or hope out into the world, ready for it to take root and grow into a more joyful experience or an even bigger dream. It's amazing what can grow from a little tiny seed or joyful thought.

Time may work against you. Don't let anything hold you back. Embrace the beauty and joy of life and live for today. Don't wait around for something that might never happen or turn down an opportunity because you think you can do it another day or don't have the time.

You can make time even if it is little and often. Take half an hour out at the beginning or end of each day for a walk, chat with a friend, or work on that project that is close to your heart. You never know where it might eventually lead. An opportunity might arise from being in the right place at the right time — what joy it will bring to yourself and others. You will feel more fulfilled when you embrace life and live in the present. Don't wait for tomorrow, live every day and shine!

You uncork the bottle and breathe in the subtle scent of dandelion — you can immediately feel your worries seep away. Just opening this potion is like bathing in daylight, making you feel hopeful and optimistic. Add a dash to a glass of water and drink in the sunshine.

Dead Sea Salt

(SALT)

Embrace fortune, create your own luck, and overcome life's challenges with resilience.

AFFIRMATION

I make my own luck and have learnt from past obstacles to build a bright and abundant future.

Your luck is in and good things are on the horizon. Remember that you are the salt of the earth and deserve all the good luck coming your way. Embrace this time and make the most of the opportunities and fortuitous situations that present themselves to you. Instead of immediately saying no to something because you think you are too busy or don't have enough time, think twice. It might present you with a new opportunity or have an outcome you never expected. You can create your own luck if you just look out for it and embrace new experiences. Good things will always come to those who wait and to those who are honest and true to themselves.

You may think lousy luck plagues you, but just remember you can make your own fortune. All you need to do is change your mindset and believe in the good. Bad things will always happen — it's all in how you perceive and deal with life's challenges. Let the good outweigh the bad, and realise that life's obstacles only make you stronger and ready to face the challenges that life throws you. Thus, you come out of all that you have weathered the master of your own destiny. Having conquered all that has been thrown at you, you can now recognise and take pride in all that you have achieved.

When life throws you a major curveball, or even a series of smaller ones, it is because you are not on your true path. This next big challenge presents itself when it is time for a change. Sometimes you need to be redirected to help you find your soul purpose. Time for reflection is required in this instance. Rebuild your life or fortify yourself so you are able to appreciate what's reaching out to you. It may appear that bad luck is following you around, but in actual fact it is just the universe's way of saying you aren't heading in the right direction.

You will learn so much more from life's challenges, and gain strength and resilience during these times. You are stronger than you think. When you change your mindset and find the positive from the (perceived) negatives, it will turn everything you believe on its head. A realisation there is actually something better out there for you. Embrace the changes or obstacles and see them as opportunities for personal growth, rather than a series of unfortunate events. Remember, you are the pioneer of your own life!

Explorers have set sail on many a deadly quest, braving the high seas to find just the right type of sea salt for this potion. Collected from the shores of the Dead Sea and distilled by alchemists, this potion purifies and protects. Starfish would cling to the ships, offering guidance and protection, even plugging the odd hole on the boat, proving good fortune for sailors.

Deadly Nightshade

(SILVER/EARTH)

*Stay focused, beware, let go,
and embrace the good.*

AFFIRMATION

I am on my true path and will not be distracted
from getting to my destination.

Don't get thrown off course. Stay on your current path and all will become clear and lead to fruition. It's all too easy to be knocked off course and letting unnecessary things distract you won't do you any good in the long run. Remember, it is easy to be led astray by beautiful things so don't let your judgement be clouded and shade you from your true path. Keep your focus and carry along the way you have set for yourself, and all will be well. Ignore unwanted distractions and things that might hurt you or slow you down from the progress you have made. Focus on your destination and you will get to where you need to be.

The most deadly can be the most beautiful. Look out for danger and betrayal crossing your path. Don't confront or pay heed to it. If it is a person, just let them pass by under cover of darkness and drift out of your life so they cause you no harm. If they say anything hurtful just let it lie and be the bigger person. It is more about them than it is about you. Don't let their poison seep into you and distract you from the good things manifesting in your life.

Trust your instincts. When someone comes into your life making you feel uncomfortable, you do not have to give them your time. Just be polite and decline any invitations or advances. Invite a friend along for company if you know you are likely to bump into them.

They will help diffuse the situation and stop you being their only focus. You will soon find they will give up and move on if you don't react to any conflict they may cause. They no doubt revel in drama, and if you don't give them any, they will most likely get bored with you and find it elsewhere.

A deadly poison kept on the highest shelf. The old apothecary shakily reaches out to the bottle when it tumbles from the shelf and smashes to the floor, scattering its contents behind the counter. The apothecary recoils. It's a warning or a promise of falsehood. The label reads: "One drop of Belladonna in each eye to see your true path and see through any betrayal. Only use on a full moon."

DIGITALIS

(COPPER)

Trust your resilience, protect your heart, and rely on your intuition to overcome challenges.

AFFIRMATION

I have healed my heart and found my inner strength. I am a fighter, courageous and compassionate.

On the surface, everything may be beautiful, but delve a little deeper and foxgloves are poisonous to the unwary. But delve deeper still, and digitalis can be a lifesaver.

You have faced adversity and can handle everything that has been thrown at you with grace and courage. You have the ability to heal yourself and repair a broken heart or mind. It may just take some time with regular doses of kindness to yourself. Don't be afraid to blow your own trumpet. You have endured a lot and are coming out the other side. Be proud of yourself. You have all you need to succeed and come out on top once again.

You have great strength of heart and a huge amount of compassion and empathy towards others, but don't let this be your downfall. Do not give your heart out too freely to others whose intentions may be insincere. Empaths need to be wary as they can give too freely and be susceptible to a broken heart. You are easily hurt and find it hard to heal. You will know deep down whose hearts are true and who might hurt you.

Trust your judgement and your intuition to break any spells cast over you. Be mindful of how people make you feel in their presence. When you feel jittery and on edge, there is usually a reason for it. You will find yourself feeling more relaxed and sure of yourself around people with good intentions.

Always trust your gut and listen to what your body is trying to tell you. It will help keep your heart whole and save you from potential anguish.

A wise woman, a herbalist, a simple woman they call the dark witch wanders the hills and forests collecting the herbs and remedies she needs to heal. Her basket is full to the brim with all manner of plants and seeds ready to dry and chop up for her stores. She carefully adds the colourful foxglove trumpets to her basket. Symbolising pride, insecurity, and intuition, this potion can heal the heart. But use it sparingly, for too much can be deadly.

Dragon's Breath

(FIRE)

Embrace the fiery spirit within as you navigate through challenges, for they hold the promise of significant transformation.

AFFIRMATION

With the dragon's breath, I unleash my inner fire and revive my soul. I feel brave and powerful.

Your spirit is on fire. You may be just coming to the end of a difficult period, so be ready to embrace the light and your newfound fiery spirit. The greater your recent challenges, the greater the reward. Be prepared for a significant transformation. The dragon has immense alchemical power. Alchemy is the process of turning lead into gold — if you've been feeling heavy and weighed down, now is the time for you to shed the load and shine. Like you, gold is rare. You radiate power and energy and can attract great things into your life when you show others your true, magnetic personality.

Be careful not to get greedy. Dragons are powerful beings and guardians, often guarding (and hoarding) treasure. However, treasure is not always material. Instead, it can be spiritual and residing deep inside your core. You just need to let it out to unleash your inner fire and potential on the world, bringing you good fortune and abundance.

Use your breath to focus on your own strength and power. Sit comfortably. Take a deep and lengthy breath in through your nose. Breathe out through your mouth more quickly than you inhaled, making a roaring sound as you forcefully expel the air from your lungs. If you want some extra oomph, open your eyes wide and stick out your tongue as you do this.

Repeat this a few times. You will feel revitalised and powerful when you embrace the dragon's breath.

The alchemist works in their laboratory. A true visionary, their work process may seem chaotic and fiery. Still, there is order in their chaos as they use the dragon's fiery breath to turn lead into gold. The dragon brings change and spirituality to the process.

Dreamcatcher

Avoid overwhelm and prioritise rest and your dreams.

AFFIRMATION

I dream big! I can achieve anything I set my mind to.

Get lots of rest and don't try to do too much at once. Sometimes we must prioritise what is most important and not try to do it all. You can achieve so much when well rested, so concentrate on manifesting that one big dream. You can achieve anything you set your mind to. The dreams we have are the realities that are waiting for us, we just have to believe it can happen and work single-mindedly towards that goal.

To help manifest the thing you dream about the most, take some time to create a vision board. Collect images that inspire you and pin or stick them to a board or a large sheet of paper. A vision board is a visual representation of your dreams, so hang it somewhere prominent where you can see it. Looking at it every day encourages you to make your dreams happen and help steer your subconcious thoughts in the right direction to achieve your dreams. Think of your vision board as your own tailored version of a dreamcatcher.

Having bad dreams or restless sleep? Hang a dreamcatcher above your bed to chase away bad dreams or negative or anxious thoughts invading your dreams and keeping you from a restful sleep. Alternatively, drink a cup of chamomile tea to promote calm and aid restfulness before you sleep. Or hang some lavender sprigs above your bed or sprinkle a few drops of lavender oil on a pillow. Consider also keeping any digital devices or phones out of your bedroom. After a few days or even a week, you might just wake up feeling less overwhelmed and more rested, ready to face each brand-new day with a revived spirit and enthusiasm. Having chased away sleepless nights, you now wake up with a new clarity and everyday twinkle in your eye.

A shaman sits weaving magic into his dreamcatchers. Placed above a bed, they are ready to capture the dreams and spirits of those who visit at night. They then channel those captured spirits into their potions to promote good dreams and chase away nightmares, being careful which dreams to bottle and which to discard. Add a few drops to your nighttime tea to promote good sleep and a restful night.

Elixir of Life

(PHILOSOPHER'S STONE)

Embrace life fully, but remember to find balance and rest when needed.

AFFIRMATION

I embrace every day as if it's my last, so I live life to the fullest.

Live your best life. You can have the time of your life at any age if only you embrace life to the fullest. Life isn't just to be lived by the young. If you look after yourself and get into good habits then the world is your oyster. If you haven't been feeling so great lately, feeling a little tired or rundown, take some time out. Get out in the fresh air. Do some exercise. The endorphins will spur you on and uplift you, encouraging you to create better habits. You can put this newfound energy into living life to the fullest.

Don't end up overdoing it. Life is full of ebbs and flows and it's okay to take time out to recharge and take care of yourself before life's next big adventure. Sometimes we can try and do a bit too much when a bit of rest is all we need. A little tonic or some self-care can instantly uplift you and add some much-needed magic to your life.

You take your life in your hands when concocting this particular potion. Alchemists have collected ingredients from the far reaches and risked their lives to brew them. Use it wisely for it is rare and hard to procure — but worth its weight in gold. One drop extends a life for one day; a whole bottle, and you'll live for an eternity.

Fairy Liquid

(AIR)

Beware of deception and seek support from trusted friends to find clarity and rejuvenation.

AFFIRMATION

My friends are a blessing; we look out for each other and enjoy time together to recharge and support each other.

Everyone needs a fairy godmother and yours is looking out for you and guiding you into the light. If life has been getting you down and you feel more Cinders than Cinderella, leave those dirty dishes and chores behind for a while.

It's time to enjoy moments with friends and take a much-needed break. A friend may offer the clarity you need and a new perspective on something troubling you. You don't always have to go it alone. It is okay to ask for help.

A change of scene, a pampering session or a day out might be just what you need. You will feel lighter and more energised for taking time out or offloading your troubles to a friend.

Remember, fairies can be mischievous and someone may be about to burst your bubble. Look out for devious tricksters that might fool or lull you into a false sense of security. Trouble might just be bubbling up and something slippery might be heading your way. Keep your true friends close and all will be well.

When you are in the midst of something or trouble is brewing, you may be too close to it to have a clear perspective or unable to see the light.

A friend who knows you well can cast fresh eyes over a situation and may just save you from yourself. Taking you back to a time when you feel free and easy again.

This little fairy is hard to contain. Light and airy, she pops out when you least expect it to guide and shine her glittery light upon you. She spreads good wishes and light wherever she goes, along with a little bit of fairy mischief. This potion is ready to pop, so don't shake it up whatever you do. Or maybe a shake up is just what you do need. The cork is likely to pop right off and release this enigmatic fairy.

Good Fortune

(GOLD)

Embrace your true nature and you will overcome obstacles and unlock your potential.

AFFIRMATION

I am my own spiritual alchemist and manifest my own gold and Elixir of Life. I am ready to embrace my full potential and purest self along with the positivity and good fortune they bring into my life.

Do you feel obstacles are in the way of your success and wellbeing? Allow yourself to overcome these obstacles and find your essence to embrace your true purpose. Don't be afraid to ask for help if obstacles are standing in your way. It may also help to break down your problem into smaller bite-sized chunks.

Trust your abilities and remember you do not have to tackle everything alone or all at once. Another person may help you unlock the potential within you that you need to succeed. Remember, a problem shared is a problem halved. You must embody your truest and most authentic self to make good things happen.

Take a deep breath, focus on your inner feelings and seek out the obstacles holding you back. What are they? Where do they come from? What do you need to remove them? Allow the wisdom and clarity that lies within yourself to float to the surface — is it best to plot a course around, over, or under them? As you slowly exhale, let go of the negative thoughts holding you back. When you focus on positive thoughts, your outlook on life will alter, and the good fortune or abundance you seek will come to you. Embrace this ultimate sense of transformation and you will meet your own potential and purest essence.

Goldfish swim in a dark pool, their essence sparkling in the cool, clear water. An ancient alchemist reaches in and deftly captures the essence in a delicate glass bottle. As it's bottled, the liquid changes from turquoise to a rich gold, signifying abundance and good fortune.

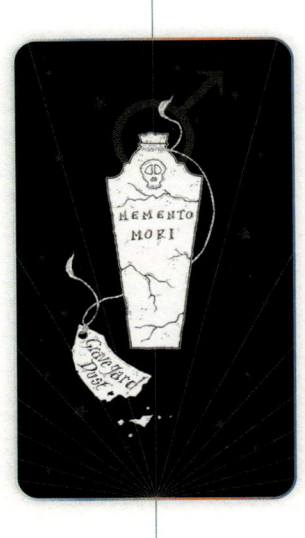

Graveyard Dust

(ASHES/EARTH)

Embrace endings as opportunities for growth and renewal.

AFFIRMATION

I live for today. I am fully present and embrace life as it is now, as well as what will be.

The end of an era is in sight. Remember, everything must reach its conclusion before a new cycle can begin, like the colourful blossoms of spring emerging from the cold grasp of winter. Whether it is something you don't quite want to end or the end of a bad spell, remember everything has its time. Bigger and better things may be ahead or on their way to you.

The good may not always outweigh the bad, but know that it won't last. Reflect on when you felt reluctant to let go of a treasured memory or eagerly welcomed the end of a challenging phase. Show gratitude for what you have by savouring each moment and cherishing the people and experiences that shape your existence.

Memento mori is a reminder to not dwell on our mortality, and to seize every opportunity in life — a reminder to not waste precious time, and be grateful for what you have. The end of something may be looming, but this means you can be reborn, ready to embrace something new or even have the opportunity to discover a better version of yourself. Doing so gives you inner peace and the resilience to navigate endings and new beginnings with a deeper appreciation for life's journey.

*The graveyard is deathly quiet and still as the grave digger makes their way through the tombstones which stand out starkly in the moonlight. On one particular gravestone, the words **'memento mori'** reflect in the moonlight. As they bow their head in silent respect, they take a pouch from their belt and gently scrape some dust from the grave into a tombstone-shaped receptacle. A potion for when all seems deathly and disastrous. To use, scatter the contents at your feet while turning in a full circle. The dust will promote growth and renewal so you are ready to embrace what comes next.*

Lightning Bolt

(PHOSPHORUS)

Seize the moment and unleash your brilliance.

AFFIRMATION

I am a bright spark of creative energy ready to set my soul on fire and thunder towards my goals.

It's time! Lightning doesn't strike in the same place twice, so take full advantage of your eureka moment. Lightning is essentially a bright spark where the positive and negative collide. You are that bright spark of energy, and however fleeting that moment might be, you can make a lasting impact and make yourself heard. After all, thunder always comes after the lightning strike — so thunder towards those goals after that initial spark of genius, as it has the power to create lasting impact and propel you towards your goals.

Even if you are still a little unsure where and when lightning might strike, it is time to go out into the world and make things happen. Waiting for inspiration to strike or something exciting to happen will only delay you. Use that nervous energy for good — it will send off sparks of inspiration and you might just collide with someone or something that sets your soul on fire.

Thunder rumbles and lightning crackles across the sky,
highlighting a tall, imposing figure in the dark.
As the storm rains down around the enigmatic magician,
the lightning bolt is channelled into a tiny receptacle.
The little bottle crackles and sparks with power.

The bright spark of energy reverberates around its tiny prison, barely containing it. Be cautious when ready to release, as a small spark can bring great things crashing down. The momentum charges around the bottle but with nowhere to go ... for now.

Lily of the Valley

(EARTH/SALT)

True happiness stems from a pure heart, and it follows from within.

AFFIRMATION

I dig deep inside myself to find my inner happiness and therefore can take it wherever I go, no matter how much life challenges me.

The path ahead of you may have been a little tricky recently and you might need to dig deep to find yourself again, but be assured good times are just around the corner. Live life with sincerity and goodness, and happiness will follow you wherever you go.
Those with a pure heart and good intentions will always live peacefully and at one with others. When you suffer from an impure heart or doubt yourself, consider what you could do to feel better. Perhaps you can do something for someone else. Help out a friend or even try volunteering at a local charity or organisation. Giving someone a well-meaning compliment can make them happy and make you feel good about yourself, too.

You will find when you are giving and sharing, it will come back on you. You may be invited out more, or receive a compliment in return. Be encouraged and before you know it, you will have created a protective circle around yourself where you feel at peace, safe, and loved. You'll feel younger and more vital when you embrace the good things in life. Just remember, lily of the valley is a tough and reliable little plant which can cover much ground — and so can you!

On the other hand, you may be taken for granted for what you do. Perhaps you are doing plenty for others but feeling underappreciated. Recognise that you are a good person with good intentions, and give yourself a well-deserved pat on the back. You don't need others to recognise all the virtuous things you do. You know in yourself you are a positive, kind person who helps others. Embrace happiness wherever you find it; remember, only you can truly make yourself happy. Don't rely on others to do this for you, for true happiness comes from within. Others will see this in you and will be drawn to your free-spirited and happy nature.

A little fairy sits quietly on the stem of the flower, drinking in pure happiness from one of the plant's tiny flower cups. There are no bad spirits in this garden, just the pure and happy spirit of the fairies. Add a few drops to a cup of water and feel the happiness and good spirits seep into your very core.

Liquid Moonlight

(SILVER)

Embrace change like the moon's phases, discover your true self.

AFFIRMATION

I embrace my feminine energy to discover who I truly am and my innermost desires. I am renewed.

Change is inevitable, so why wait! Just like the Moon, we go through different phases and cycles. The Moon and its feminine energy can guide us through darker times to a period of enlightenment, leading us to make the changes we so desperately need. Embrace your innermost desires and allow yourself to discover who you truly are. You can't stop the rhythm of time or the shifting of the tide, but you can embrace change and better connect with yourself and your changing emotions. Being idle and sedentary is not in our nature so keep flowing and moving and progressing through life.

Don't eclipse your needs for the needs of others. You can't help anyone without looking after yourself first. Make the changes you need first, so you will be better equipped to face what life throws at you and help others if you do.

A mysterious bottle gleams silver as if the very Moon itself is in the room, inviting the visitor to reach out and claim the potion for themselves. The label reads, 'liquid moonlight'. One drop on the tongue is plenty, for your intuition will do the rest. The visitor does not take heed and takes a large swig.

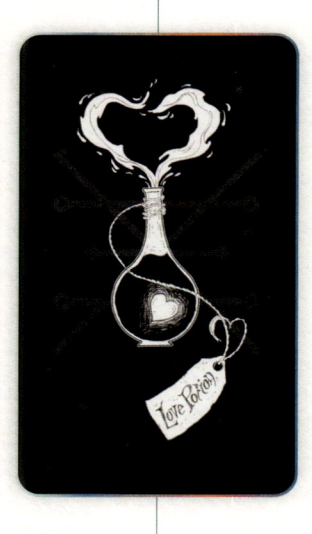

Love Potion

(COPPER)

Be open to love, and focus on self-love before finding the perfect partner.

AFFIRMATION

I let love into my life by loving myself first and embracing those who choose to come into my life as it is.

Love is in the air! Embrace your inner goddess and your sparkly personality will shine out, attracting others to you. Show them what an amazing person you are and how lucky they are to have you in their life. Be open to letting another person into your life; you never know what might happen. You don't want to miss out on something extraordinary and lasting with that special someone — so keep your head up, be confident, and smile. You never know who you might meet or when.

Love potions can be powerful, so use them wisely. It's all too easy to become infatuated with someone who isn't right for you or doesn't want a relationship. If your feelings are not reciprocated and it all seems too hard, it might be time to move on and focus on the love you have for yourself instead. Take some time out at the end of each day to look after yourself. Take a bath, pamper yourself or do something you enjoy like reading a book or going for a walk in nature. It might just help you find some peace and regain your sense of self.

Remember, it is okay to treat or reward yourself once in a while. Try leaving yourself little love notes around the house to remind you of what you love about yourself or your life, or write it down in a journal. Turn the music up on a favourite song and let yourself loose. Dancing around the house can give you the feel-good factor and release endorphins, a way to awaken your inner goddess.

And remember to have a lasting, healthy relationship, you must love yourself and your life first. The perfect partner will only be drawn to your confidence and add to the life you already love.

With a dash of desire and a pinch of passion, this potion is concocted by Venus and handed on to Cupid to distribute wisely. Beware: a little bit goes a long way, so a few drops could cause serious infatuation or heartache. Use sparingly and let Cupid do his job.

Mandrake Root

(EARTH/WATER)

Embrace new projects patiently, and wait for the right moment to leap forward.

AFFIRMATION

I am ready to nurture the essential things in my life and let them grow and flourish.

Now is the time to birth a new project or start a new chapter in your family or working life. Whatever you are planning will grow into something wonderful. Like anything that needs a little nurturing, it might take a little time and effort, but keep going and all will come to fruition. Make whatever it is you would like to achieve a personal goal. Set aside time each day or once a week to work on the plans you have set yourself. Once the seed has been sown, there is no holding you back. Before you know it, the little seed will have turned into something mighty and precious to you.

Don't uproot your life too much — it could lead to disaster and the death of your well-thought-out plans. Screaming and shouting and making a fuss will do you no good. Play it out. It's just not the right time for a big move or leap into the unknown. Sometimes you just have to be patient. It might be there are circumstances in your life holding you back right now. It could be small things making delays or larger, major life events that are stunting your growth and your well-thought-out plans. You can still take small steps, but you don't have to overwhelm yourself. You don't want things to break down completely because you have taken on too much, too soon. If you are frustrated with slow progress, remember, once the time is right you will be an unstoppable force because you have nurtured yourself in anticipation of what is to come.

Harvesting mandrake root is a dangerous business, so it's best left to the professionals. Earmuffs are a must, as these plants can cause anything from temporary deafness to death. According to legend, a mandrake root when dug up screams so loudly it can drive the listener mad or kill all who hear it. Place a small chunk under your pillow to grow something wonderful while you slumber.

Mermaid's Song

(DIAMOND)

*Embrace your inner siren and
break free from judgement.*

AFFIRMATION

I dance to my own tune. I am fierce and
strong and let my individuality shine through.

You are a siren and at your most potent. You have let others walk over you for far too long, but now it's time to let out your inner femme fatale and stop bowing to those who may be judging or stifling your talents. You don't have to conform to what others think you should be. Let your individuality and wild magic out. You may have felt stifled for quite some time or a little inhibited. Show people who you really are, and embrace your creative and enigmatic self.

You have never been a follower but a trendsetter. You just need the confidence to shine and embrace your feminine. If you want to wear the flamboyant outfit or favourite hat, then just wear it. Walk out with confidence, with your head held high, and you could see things from a startling new perspective — even receive a compliment or two. Watch how people are drawn to your newfound confidence and feminine spirit and the new friends and opportunities that come your way. Remember you have a fierce, strong, and independent spirit. Transform yourself to live life how you want to live it.

The siren's song is haunting and powerful. Just because you can walk all over someone or lure someone in with your charms doesn't mean you should. You don't need to trample those in your path. You can always just help them on their way instead. Use your charms to do good, and above all, be kind.

You can't help but attract people towards you with your magnetic personality. It's a wonderful trait to possess and can bring all manner of opportunities and potential your way. However, be careful — you could also attract unwanted attention. Be mindful of what you encourage, as it is possible you could land yourself in a tempestuous situation. Perhaps someone may want to spend more time with you than you want to spend with them. You don't want to hurt anyone's feelings or cause any rifts, so be gentle with other people's feelings, and above all, be honest and true to yourself. In turn, your integrity will shine through to others and show them you are genuine, stopping any judgement or unease in its tracks.

A beautiful mermaid curls up seductively. As she stares deep into your eyes—the windows of your soul—she begins to sing. Her harmonies reach deep into the recesses of your mind, overpowering your senses and making you tingle all over. You look away, breaking the spell and capturing her essence. The haunting melody is now just a low hum coming from the bottle you carefully place in your pocket. This potion will knock anyone off their feet and make a woman feel like a goddess.

Mermaid's Tears

(GOLD/SILVER)

Embrace the natural ebb and flow of emotions and find renewal and fulfilment in any state.

AFFIRMATION

I will embrace the highs and lows that flow into my life and come out the other side revitalised and ready to face whatever life brings.

Sometimes our mood or energy is high and sometimes it is low. Like the waxing and waning of the Moon, we grow stronger and weaker in waves. Everything comes full circle.

If you are feeling low, it is okay to let the healing tears flow — embrace the renewal of spirit this release brings. Do what you must to let all the emotions come forth, whether sobbing into a pillow or being moved by a sad film or a song. Accept the sacred feminine spirit of the mermaid and let her healing powers into your heart. Don't let feelings grow stagnant — let them float to the surface and be carried away with the tide, leaving you refreshed and revitalised.

If your mood is high, make the most of the mermaid's playful spirit and your own vitality. Dance, go out with friends, or do something bold and blissful. This is the time to celebrate the sea goddess' charm.

Get out into the world and show off your best self and the amazing energy and creativity the goddess has brought you. When you do this, you're still letting your emotions flow aligned, leaving you feeling light and fulfilled.

———— ✴ ————

A lone mermaid sits on a rock in the moonlight weeping for her lost love. She knows the power of her own tears, so she swiftly captures them in a vial which hangs around her neck. Alchemists would fall at a mermaid's feet for what is in that bottle. For mermaid's tears are potent and powerful with healing properties.

Night Owl Potion

(SILVER)

*Embrace emerging clarity and allow
your inner wisdom to guide you.*

AFFIRMATION

I am a leader and independent thinker capable of
making decisions to light up my true path.

You are coming out of the darkness and into the light. Harness your emerging clarity by utilising your wit and wisdom. You are an independent thinker who can achieve anything you put your mind to. You just have to work smart — don't be in a rush. Take your time to carefully observe, listen, and assess, allowing yourself to make informed decisions. Trust your intuitive nature, often described as an 'old soul', as it holds ancient wisdom to guide you along your chosen path. By doing so, you will inevitably discover the illuminating light of success and fulfilment ahead.

Don't let your light go out or be dimmed by others. You don't need others to drag you from your perch. You have the wisdom and insight to lead and show others the way. You might not think it but you are a leader and independent thinker. You don't have to follow the flock. Fly solo and spread your wings wide! By listening to your inner wisdom, you will be guided towards transformative experiences, meaningful connections, and a sense of purpose that aligns with your soul's calling.

A wise owl nestles in the dark, his effervescent globe-like eyes are the only indication of his presence. The owl stretches, and with one swift movement launches into the night leaving a lone feather fluttering down in the darkness. Down this potion in one to activate your inner wisdom.

Octopus Ink

Simplify your life by letting go of excessive commitments and free your energy for what matters most.

AFFIRMATION

I am creative, intelligent, and well-equipped to handle all that life throws me. I thrive when I do things for myself.

When you are juggling too much and have your fingers in too many pies, you will inevitably drop the ball. It's wise to let something go before everything falls apart. You don't have to do it all alone — ask for help. Delegate or relinquish a project that isn't filling your tank before you are wiped out and completely overwhelmed, unable to do anything at all. When you do, you create space for yourself, the chance to fill your tank again and have the energy you need to lead a fulfilling life.

You are at risk of blending into your surroundings and disappearing entirely. You feel unseen and underappreciated. Put out feelers and do something for yourself, instead of for other people. Make a splash and get yourself noticed. Something that will inspire you and make you stand out again. You have the ability to multitask and regenerate — use it! Challenge yourself and reap the rewards.

The octopus undulates through the water. At first, he is unaware of the presence below him and prepares to strike with his inky defences. The viscous black liquid whirlpools into the water, enveloping the scene in darkness. The hunter is adept to these conditions and deftly bottles the inky substance. No need to water this potion down — it has already been diluted.

Phoenix Fire

(FIRE)

Empower yourself to embrace change, face adversity, and unlock your hidden potential.

AFFIRMATION

I rise from the ashes like a beautiful, fiery phoenix and embrace all the new and wonderful opportunities coming my way.

You are yearning for change. Now is the time to try something new or set a new goal. By taking this potion and embracing the power of the phoenix, you ignite your inner fire, take on its courage, and have the energy to face anything that life throws at you.

When you're feeling anxious, *Phoenix Fire* gives you the strength to persevere. Cast your fears aside and acknowledge that adversity makes you stronger. You will come out the other side feeling renewed and hopeful. A phoenix is unique and individual. It has everything it needs to regenerate and heal — just like you have everything within you to set your soul on fire.

A phoenix has to wither and die to become reborn into its new life. Life is cyclical, including our moods and our energy. Now is the time to tap into this cycle and feel re-energised and ready to face a bright new dawn. Seek opportunities for renewal, whether it is exploring new interests, acquiring fresh knowledge, or pursuing a different path. Embrace the transformative power of alchemy and allow it to guide you toward a brilliant new future.

The call of the phoenix brings great changes. Embracing their fire infuses you with courage, resilience, and an unwavering spirit. As you release your fears, you will unlock your hidden potential and witness the transformative magic within you. Prepare to rise from the ashes and embrace a life filled with purpose, fulfilment, and a profound connection to your innermost being.

The energy of the fiery phoenix thrums inside the bottle, waiting to be unleashed, its flaming feathers swirling inside. The phoenix's energy is powerful, so be ready to absorb all that firepower — this is a one-hit wonder. The phoenix represents rebirth and renewal, which is just what you get when you consume the fire within.

Poison

(SAND OF TIME)

Protect yourself from toxic influences, trust your intuition, and maintain your inner strength.

AFFIRMATION

I choose only to consume what is beneficial to me and have the antidote within me to fight off poisonous effects.

Don't let another's poisonous intent knock you out.
Some people are toxic and narcissistic by nature.
You are sensitive, and poisonous types are drawn to your kindness and empathy. Don't let them drain you of your life force. If need be, sever ties with these people or take some time out to recharge so you have the antidote to fight off their adverse effects when you meet them again.

Trust your intuition — you have a sixth sense and will know who is good for you and who is not in an instant. Protect yourself at all costs. The more you trust your intuition, the more instinctive it will become. Like the poison taster, you will be able to sense when something is amiss before you even taste it — a sixth sense for those who might do you harm. Your life will be better and more peaceful when you trust your instincts. Having the ability to avoid harmful situations before anything takes hold will make your life more stable and tranquil. When you are secure in yourself, it makes it much harder for others to taint you with their poison or drag you down.

If the poison has already taken hold, remove yourself from the unpleasant situation. Spend some time alone to recharge, or visit friends who build you up and fortify you, rather than those who bring you down and take advantage of your sweetness. Remember, you have the power to say "no" and to avoid letting the poison seep in.

And you can do it with compassion and kindness too. Keep yourself busy in other ways so you don't have time to dwell on these people. Having true friends around you will add a protective, warm, and fuzzy layer to your life, making it so much more peaceful and enjoyable. Take time out to recharge and collect yourself, so you feel stronger and able to repel the toxic effects of others with ease and grace.

A poison taster sits in their chamber surrounded by poisons, of all different strengths and effectiveness. But this little vial simply labelled 'Poison' is the most deadly of them all. Just unstopping the vial could down a person at a hundred paces. They pocket the little bottle ...

Poison Ivy

(SAND OF TIME)

Take time to appreciate where you are and choose your path wisely.

AFFIRMATION

I must use this time wisely and embrace all new experiences to make the most of my transformation and nurture what will come.

Ivy most often wards the edges of a forest; do you apply caution and take it as a sign that none should pass? Or, keep on going and end up in a sticky thicket or bad situation? Are you even on the correct path?

If you are, enjoy the scenery and remember to stop once in a while, rest, and take some time to enjoy all the bounty there is to offer. Stop and smell the flowers and take in the beauty of your surroundings. Life is not always about getting to a final outcome or destination. You must remember to live for today. The little moments are just as important as the big life events and can be just as joyful and memorable. Don't regret not making each day count while constantly chasing an uncertain 'bigger and better' future.

Finding a path filled with poison ivy may suggest that you have taken a wrong turn and are not in harmony with nature or yourself. Stop! Reassess where you are going and you will find it will lead you to a new exciting place. Why not make a bucket list of things you would like to achieve or incorporate into your life. Then assess whether what you are currently doing is going to lead you to these places or accomplishments. If not, then it might be time to move in a different direction.
It could be something small like taking up a new hobby, or it could be a more drastic change, for instance, a new job or career path.

Remember, it is okay to change your mind if you feel the path you have taken so far isn't the right one. Imagine how it will feel to begin ticking things off your bucket list, and how fulfilled and exhilarated you will feel.

The herbalist enters the sanctuary of their lush and exotic greenhouse. This is not just a pretty garden, but a deadly one. A poison garden, lethal to the untrained. At the very back of the garden is a hidden workshop with shelves cluttered with various deadly and rare potions. Procured and brewed over the master's lifetime from their most poisonous botanicals. The hidden workshop is protected by delicate tendrils of ivy. As they approach, the tightly wrapped tendrils fall away revealing a hidden door. The ivy protecting what is inside from outsiders, transforming only for the herbalist.

Pumpkin Juice

(EARTH)

Embrace abundance, but stay vigilant and surround yourself with positivity.

AFFIRMATION

I treat myself kindly and surround myself with loved ones. Tricksters be gone!

Treat yourself. It's a time for great possibilities and abundance. Try something new, do something fun, be open to a unique experience. Something magical and wonderful might happen or a great wish of yours might be fulfilled. But remember, you have to get out amongst the harvest to reap the rewards of the crop. Organise some time out and spend time with friends. Go out to dinner, or throw caution to the wind and host a party. It doesn't have to be a major life event to organise something fun. Embrace your inner child and get out in the fresh air, run into the sea, or throw some autumn leaves around until you fall down. Exhausted but happy. Just get in on the action!

Beware the trickster. Someone may be out to wreak havoc around you. Ward off these evil spirits by shining your jack-o'-lantern light bright and surrounding yourself with positivity and generosity of spirit. In other words, keep your friends and family close, they will protect and look out for you. You will feel protected and loved, and bad intentions won't even get a second glance but bounce off all the happy energy you have created for yourself.

The cork comes out with an effervescent 'pop' releasing an earthy undertone and then that delightful pumpkin flavour. May make you hiccup. Share with your friends for a riotous old time. Trick or treat!

Rainbow Dust

(GOLD)

Embrace the magic of rainbows and find optimism in life's ups and downs.

AFFIRMATION

Life is full of promise and good times are here to stay. I only have to make it so.

When you see a rainbow arcing across the sky, you can't help but feel optimistic and that life is full of promise. A rainbow promises sunshine after the rain — good times are on their way. Maybe even an elusive pot of gold. Gold doesn't have to represent money but also attraction and magnetic personalities. It might be someone coming into your life or even representing your shiny and sparkly self. A rainbow promises better times to come.

Remember that you will never experience a rainbow without the rain. To appreciate the good times we have to go through the bad. The bad times will always come and go — it is how we live and learn from them that matters. It makes us appreciate the good times all the more. It is far too easy to dwell on the negatives in life, particularly if you feel that the bad keeps on coming at you.

Sometimes we have to teach ourselves to look on the bright side to realise there is more good in our lives than we think. Practising gratitude helps. Actively acknowledge and appreciate the good things that happen. It can help to write these down in a journal, or thank those in life by expressing your gratitude out loud. Look for the silver linings. Be optimistic — rather than letting the rain weigh your mood down, choose to dance in it instead.

A potion that is impossible to find and almost as impossible to bottle. Made by leprechauns in deepest, darkest Ireland — a magical and enchanted land steeped in myth and legend. Only a leprechaun can find the pot of gold at the end of a rainbow, so only a leprechaun can bottle its dust. Leprechauns are solitary and live in remote places so almost impossible to reach, never mind the rainbow. With a bit of added mischief their optimism knows no bounds, so treasure these creatures and their potions. Don't let it go to waste.

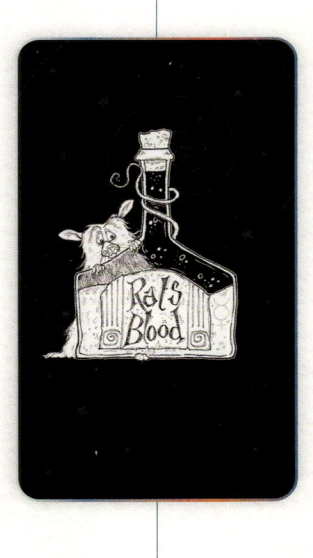

Rats' Blood

(MERCURY)

Find fulfilment in simplicity, balance ambition with gratitude, and thrive towards success.

AFFIRMATION

I live every day with gratitude and I am happy with my life. I strive to be the best I can be and improve my situation.

It is the beginning of a new dawn and great success is within your grasp, but beware of those who may hinder your progress. Some individuals may judge, betray, or deceive you as you approach your achievements. Exercise caution in trusting others and sharing your plans. The rat's quick-thinking, witty intelligence, along with its agile nature, can teach us so much.

Sometimes it is the simple things in life that can bring us the most peace and contentment. Being happy with what you have and living every day with gratitude is the first step, but this doesn't mean we can't have ambition and strive or reach out for more.

Be careful who you trust — there are those who might stand in your way. They may try to judge you because you are on the verge of success, or be disloyal or deceitful. Be careful what you share with others. Surround yourself with loyal and supportive individuals who genuinely have your best interests at heart.

By embracing the rat's wisdom and heeding the advice, you will safeguard your journey to success. With discernment and careful choices, you can shield yourself from judgement, betrayal, and deceit. Balancing gratitude with ambition will bring you inner peace, contentment, and a supportive network that propels you toward your goals, ensuring a fulfilling and prosperous path ahead.

Love them or loathe them, rats are occasionally revered trickster deities and messengers. Not one for drinking, but add it to your cauldron and let the steam envelop you. Promotes clear or quick thinking and other qualities the enigmatic rat can teach us.

Revive

PHILOSOPHER'S STONE

Embrace vitality, prioritise self-revival, and thrive in purposeful living.

AFFIRMATION

I am fully present in my own life
and feel revived and energised.

You are finally feeling on top of the world and fighting fit after a period of low energy and lethargy. Things are looking up and you feel revived and rejuvenated. Take advantage of this time and go out into the world radiating your joy onto others. Go out for the day with friends, volunteer, or find a new active hobby. You can uplift and achieve so much with all this extra energy and spirit. Channel all this joy for life into something that matters to you, and it will give your life purpose, filling you with even more enthusiasm and positivity. You will be a force to be reckoned with, and others will enjoy spending time with you too. Make the most of it!

You might be feeling a little lifeless and low on energy. Life has knocked the wind out of you lately and you need a tonic. Bring yourself back into existence and take small steps to revive your body and soul so you can thrive. First, get some rest. If you can, take some time off; if not, allow yourself an hour here and there to do something you want to do. Go for a walk, read a book, or go to bed early. Ask a friend or family member for a favour to allow you some time out. Before you know it, you will have topped up your well and be feeling more present and alive. We all need to take care of our wellbeing to care for others, live our lives purposefully, and enjoy ourselves.

Leave a simple wooden cup out on a rainy night of a full moon. Collect the rainwater, then add a few drops of this potion at exactly midnight, and down the contents. Otherwise known as the 'Elixir of Life'.

Seahorse Scales

(WATER)

Reflect on your purpose — it's within your power to overcome challenges and change.

AFFIRMATION

I have the ability to get what I want from this life.
I can see the bigger picture.

Expand your awareness and consider all that is going on for you. Reflect on your true purpose — what do you really want? This potion inspires you to put steps in place for creating the life you want. It is up to you how you live, and with a little effort, you could improve your life should you choose. It might be as simple as making time for friends and family, or working on a creative project in your free time, or even saving for a holiday. Before you know it, you will have achieved a lifelong dream, or be sharing the same space as those exotic seahorses when you dip a toe into the ocean of some far-flung mysterious place.

Occasionally, you just cannot see the wood from the trees. The seahorse is a charming creature, full of charisma, helping you overcome your blocks. Look for alternative ways to overcome problems. Look to a family member or trusted friend for guidance if you just can't see a solution or the way out of a problem.

Sometimes our brains can feel so full we feel completely overwhelmed. Our turbulent thoughts chaotically tumbling around making us feel muffled like we are underwater. Try doing a brain dump — write down a list of all the things you have in your head. It might be as simple as a to-do list or writing all your thoughts in a journal. It helps to get everything on paper and out of your head.

Leave yourself space to work through the problem yourself, or show someone else what you are struggling with, so they might be able to help you. Before you know it, you have cleared your chaotic mind and taken back your power.

Collected ethically from a willing seahorse. Seahorses are intuitive creatures. They have the ability to see the past, present, and future. Steep the scales in water and sip throughout the day to promote self-awareness. An excellent potion to share with a friend for true insight.

Shroomka

(SULPHUR)

Engage in self-discovery, and seize opportunities for personal growth and transformation.

AFFIRMATION

I must use this time wisely and embrace all new experiences that make the most of my transformation and growth.

Just like when Alice met the Caterpillar in Wonderland, you are ready to embrace a spell of rapid growth. Welcome the changes that come your way and allow yourself to grow and flourish like a butterfly emerging from its cocoon. Positive changes may well be in your future; however, this growth may be short-lived, so don't waste this time or become complacent. Remember to enjoy this period of self-discovery to prolong your wellbeing and overcome any future challenges.

Embrace the momentum of growth and engage in activities that nurture your personal development. Explore new paths, acquire knowledge, and challenge yourself to expand beyond your comfort zone. Continuously seek opportunities for growth and transformation. There is nothing like finding the one thing—through exploration—that sets your soul on fire to make you grow exponentially and catapult you onto bigger and better things. By wholeheartedly embracing this phase of rapid growth, you will experience profound personal transformation and fulfilment.

Fueling that fire in your belly will provide you with a sense of clarity and a burning desire to succeed, while keeping things simmering along and fruitful when they slow down again. Utilise this time for self-discovery, and the positive changes that arise will extend beyond the present moment.

Your newfound resilience and self-awareness will serve as valuable tools to overcome future challenges, leading to an enriched and purposeful life.

A cheeky tipple brewed from a rare toadstool.
Go easy on this one, as too much in one go could prove a
gigantic mistake and make you a little tipsy. However,
a dram could be good for the soul and your wellbeing.

Sleeping Draught

(SILVER)

Rest, recharge, and find balance to prevent burnout.

AFFIRMATION

I am rested and relaxed and fully committed to creating balance in my life.

You may have been overdoing it lately. Take some time out to recuperate and recharge. When you are too busy to take time to rest, remember how much more productive and focused you can be when you are feeling rested. You can get things done much faster and without procrastination when you aren't exhausted from lack of quality rest. Incorporate more regular downtime into your routine. It will help you in the long run and bring some much needed balance into your life.

Can't seem to get on top of things no matter how much you sleep? Always feeling tired? You might be burnt out and more than a little stressed. Fresh air or some gentle exercise will do wonders to help you sleep. Make sure you get out of the house for a while during the day if you just can't switch your brain off at night or are prone to overthinking. Burn some lavender before you sleep, or put a few drops on a pillow to help you relax and unwind at night. Put a few drops into a bath with some Epsom salts (magnesium) to calm your nervous system and help promote sleep.

A little bit of rest can really turn things around. You'll wake up with more energy for the day ahead, which means you will get more done. Before you know it, you will have everything back in order and be feeling on top of the world again.

A tired worker rests in a deep and restorative sleep. An empty vial of this draught stands at his bedside and lavender is under his pillow, filling the room with its woodsy and heady scent.

Snake Venom

(MERCURY)

Harness your renewed energy and make the most of your vibrant spirit.

AFFIRMATION

I feel renewed and full of life. I channel this excess energy into something productive.

You are feeling renewed and full of energy and perhaps even a little bit restless. Put this excess energy to good use. Perhaps take up a creative hobby or try out a new activity. You may even exceed everyone else's expectations during this time and surprise yourself with how much you learn or get done. Having a sense of purpose will only make you feel even more rejuvenated and give you a sense of pride in what you have achieved.

Restless spirits can get into trouble and are easily charmed by someone slippery, so watch out for temptation and others leading you astray. We tend to rely more on others to pave our way forward when we're bored or have free time, rather than making our own choices. Be strong in your values and don't let a bad apple tempt you. You could end up a little bruised.

Put that nervous energy into something you are passionate about or which challenges you. It could be by helping someone in need, so you could volunteer at a local charity or animal shelter. Perhaps the hobby you take up means you can share more of what you create or pass knowledge onto others, helping them feel happy and fulfilled. So you are leading the way instead of letting others take the lead. Be committed to yourself—and others—and you'll be living in harmony and acceptance with all those around you.

The snake curls itself around an ancient tree, which bears the richest and most decadent fruit. The snake is cunning and tempts those who pass to eat the forbidden fruit. This could result in dire consequences, including banishment from paradise or worse. The venom in this potion is from that very snake — potent and full of temptation. Take one drop on the tip of the tongue to channel restlessness and promote renewal. Warning: Never be tempted to consume more than the allocated dose.

Spider Venom

(PENTAGRAM)

Embrace your creativity, stay open to others, and weave remarkable creations while nurturing a supportive community.

AFFIRMATION

I embrace my creativity as it is woven into all aspects of my life. I share and connect with others through my creativity.

Spiders create beautiful, intricate webs. Like them, it's time to embrace your creativity, whether it's through art, writing, music, or any other form of creative endeavour, you have the opportunity to tap into your inner world and manifest something beautiful. It doesn't have to be in a purely practical sense, it could also be spiritual. Be patient and take your time and you might just weave and manifest something truly remarkable, whether it's a piece of art or an intention. Give yourself permission to experiment, make mistakes, and learn along the way. Creativity is a process, and sometimes the best outcomes emerge when we let go of expectations and trust the journey.

Be careful not to get too caught up with yourself, for you may just get stuck in a web of your own making — over-thinking, self-doubt, or perfectionism hinders progress. Maintain a balanced perspective. Staying open to new ideas, feedback, and collaboration with others help you stay tethered to the people around you who help nurture your creativity. We are all interconnected and others may enjoy sharing or being part of your creative journey.

Maybe you can teach something to others or show them the way, being a source of inspiration for yourself and those around you. By fostering a community around your creativity, you create a space for mutual growth and support. Embrace your creativity with patience, curiosity, and a willingness to explore. Weave your webs of imagination and manifest something truly wonderful, while remembering the importance of remaining open, sharing your experiences, and inspiring others along the way.

A spider busies itself in a dark and dusty corner. Taking its time, it slowly spins its gossamer web. Seeming simple at first, the pattern becomes more and more intricate and involved. It's a beautiful creative tapestry of form and colour. Not only the spider's home but a beautiful and deadly trap for the unaware. It may seem benign until the spider appears twitching its fangs.

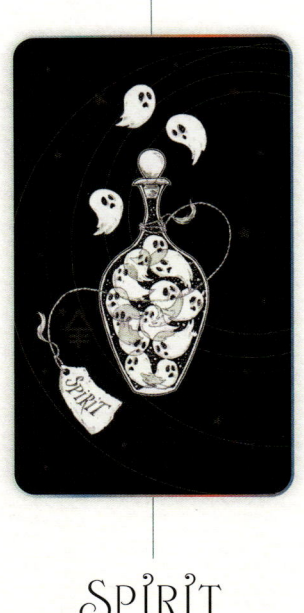

SPIRIT

(PHOSPHORUS)

Be your own spiritual alchemist and change what is base into gold.

AFFIRMATION

I will embrace my true self, releasing my potential so I can live my best life.

Sometimes anxiety takes hold and we feel trapped or inhibited. We lose our zest for life. Take a deep steadying breath and imagine your spirit is sleeping soundly in a secret box buried deep within you. To reawaken your spirit you need to unlock that box. Your negative thoughts are getting in your way and stopping you from opening the box and living your best life.

Send your breath around your body to find the key. When you find an obstacle, an anxious thought blocking your path, slowly release your breath and banish it so you can continue the search for the key. You are now starting upon a new course of heightened awareness to unveil your purest self, thus allowing you to live in the moment, freely and without obstruction. As you banish the last negative thought holding you back, the key is revealed to you.

Inhale as you turn the key, exhaling slowly as you open the box, releasing not only your breath, but your true spirit.

A controversial potion. A spirit should be free to fly, not confined in a little glass prison. However, some spirits are lost and need a little encouragement to find their way in the dark.

Stardust

(PENTAGRAM)

Embrace your cosmic energy, and achieve your dreams; but avoid burnout and stay grounded for a fulfilling life.

AFFIRMATION

You are made of stardust. Embrace your dreams and your magical potential to shine bright.

It's time to spread your badass cosmic wings! You are a pure, cosmic ball of energy. Channel that energy and make the most of this time to shine and achieve your dreams. Like a star at night, you are at your most magical and charismatic. But be cautious … Overdoing it can lead to burnout or even worse, a black hole, so take care of yourself and don't get too starry eyed. Remember to keep yourself a little grounded so you don't get lost in the ether. Balance is important in life. Take breaks when needed, prioritise self-care activities, and nurture your physical, mental, and emotional health.

There are a multitude of positive benefits from maintaining balance. Your radiance will attract opportunities and people, drawn to your magical and charismatic presence. You will feel a sense of fulfilment and achievement as you make progress towards your dreams. Moreover, by staying grounded, you will avoid getting lost in the ethereal realm and maintain a strong connection to reality, enabling you to navigate challenges with clarity and wisdom. Overall, by spreading those wings with care, you will soar to new heights and create a harmonious and fulfilling life.

Collected over centuries from fallen stars, this potion is rare and precious so use it wisely. A potion filled with magic dust, dreams, and pure energy. Sprinkle dust sparingly over yourself. Only to be used at nighttime when the stars are at their brightest.

Storm in a Bottle

(WATER/AIR)

Embrace the eye of the storm, and be ready to come out the other side.

AFFIRMATION

I am thankful for my loved ones, and I can calm the stormy chaos inside me.

Life can be stormy, and you yourself feel turbulent and more than a little chaotic. You may be feeling mystified by the direction your life is taking you and not thinking clearly. Dive deep down into the whirlpool that is your thoughts to find a sense of order and inner clarity. Take a few minutes each day to meditate. Take a deep steadying breath and let all those tempestuous thoughts settle to a quiet breeze within your mind. With each exhale, let go of the chaos that rules your mind until all feels calm again. Ultimately, be patient and ride out the storm. Your path will become apparent with time — you just need to trust you will weather the storm.

Don't let the confusion consume you and spiral you into negative thought patterns. Lack of clear thinking can lead to poor choices. Remember that stormy times can bring people together. Look to others for camaraderie and support. It's at times like these you need to know who your friends are.

You hold this potion in the palm of your hand.
Its contents swirl violently. Your grip isn't quite tight
enough and the tumultuous energy inside knocks
the bottle from your grasp. It tumbles to the ground,
shattering into a million pieces, and lets loose the chaotic

storm within. It swirls all around, your hair and robes billowing as its full power is released and the storm rages around you. You stand your ground in the eye of the storm, but know you can only hold on for so long.

Sunbeams

(GOLD)

Radiate your sunny and bright energy, unaffected by others' negativity or judgements.

AFFIRMATION

I am filled with light and boundless energy which radiates and spreads to the people around me.

The Sun is shining and life is filling you with boundless energy and positivity. You are embracing this new dawn with a newfound confidence and clarity. It is an excellent time to try something new, make new friends and get out into the world. Enjoy the current ride and take it with you wherever you go. Spreading it around and showering your bright, brilliant energy down on others. You are magnetic and draw good things to you and radiate that joy to others, improving the wellbeing of those around you. Happiness comes from within. Let it radiate and spread sunshine all around you.

Quite simply, you are so sunny and bright others may get exasperated with you. Don't let anyone dull your sparkle. Jealousy and judgement are not worth your time. While you might be feeling on top of the world right now, there will be others in your life who won't always share your feelings of positivity and joy. Don't forget to be compassionate to other people and their plights. You are strong enough to be able to lift up and encourage others with your positivity. But you also don't want to become that friend who is inadvertently rubbing everyone else up the wrong way with your constant joy, so don't let your enthusiasm run away with you.

Remember to stop and listen to others and even reign in your enthusiasm when necessary. To stop being judged, you also need to judge what is appropriate and when.

Your friends will thank you for it, and in turn, also feel supported and listened to, promoting a continued sense of wellbeing all around.

A tiny vial hangs in a dark corner. But on approach its bright light fills the room, radiating into every crack and crevice. It fills your every being with hope and positivity. You leave feeling like you have found your way in the dark and with an added radiance.

Tincture of Toad

(PHILOSOPHER'S STONE)

Navigate through challenges and obstacles to claim your well-deserved success.

AFFIRMATION

Success is within my grasp. I must take one step at a time to continually move forward and meet my goals.

The toad is leading you to the birth of your success. However, it could be slightly rocky or unsure ground, so the path may not be direct or easy, and you might feel like obstacles and hurdles are continually being thrown in your path. You might need to transform or reframe your way of thinking to overcome these challenges. So don't be too rigid, as you may need to adapt to changing circumstances. Take them as they come and realise that the things you want the most may not always come to you easily. But you will make it out the other side of the gauntlet and be able to celebrate all your hard work and success. It could take some time, and you may have to do a job or weather events you do not particularly like for a short time. Remember, brighter days follow a storm, and you will come out the other side with a new lease of life and feeling invigorated.

Beware of liars and poisonous intent. They may get in your way, and like arsenic, the exposure can slowly poison you in a battle against your own wellbeing. It is your choice whether to side-step these people or face them head-on. Do you feel equipped to take them on? Either way, make sure you have others in your corner. You don't have to fight these battles alone — support from others can work wonders.

These types of people are bullies and will always pick on those that they feel are smaller or weaker. You are neither of these things. You are resilient and strong. Let others fortify you. You may even find you forge better working or personal relationships and realise you are not the only one to come under the wrath of these individuals. All this will ultimately make you stronger and more resilient, allowing you to forge your own path ahead and meet your goals with confidence and with an impenetrable armour.

A gnarly old toad guards the entrance to a cave. Inside, jewels twinkle and treasure sparkles. Enter at your own peril, for the toad may be poisonous. The toad will not let you pass with ease; you will have to prove your worth and work hard to gain entry past this great guardian and protector. The toad's essence is a potent one, and only the worthy will get to the treasure.

Truth Serum

(COPPER)

Follow your truth, and be guided by honesty and integrity.

AFFIRMATION

I live my life with honesty and integrity and know this will lead me on a true and great path.

Follow your truth, for your authentic path is ahead.
It is a path that intertwines with honesty and integrity,
guiding you towards a life of fulfilment and purpose.
Listen to your head and your heart, and know that you
are making the correct choices that will lead you where
you need to be. You will be certain that things will work
out how they should.

As you navigate through the twists and turns, remember
the delicate dance between truth and compassion.
Never trample on others to get where you need to be.
Sometimes, a gentle white lie can shield others' feelings
without compromising your authenticity. Consider the
scenario where a loved one seeks your opinion on their
creative work; you can acknowledge their effort and offer
constructive suggestions to preserve their spirit while
uplifting their confidence.

Embracing your truth opens doors to a cascade
of positive benefits. Certainty and trust abound.
Opportunities aligned with your truth are drawn
towards you. Meaningful connections are forged, as
your unwavering commitment to honesty inspires
and transforms the lives of those around you. Honesty
becomes a beacon guiding you as you explore your true
path. When you do this, you unlock a life brimming with
purpose, fulfilment, and a profound sense of authenticity.

A powerful little potion, one that could have dire consequences in the wrong hands. One drop could tell a thousand truths or break a thousand hearts. Use wisely and sparingly.

Unicorn Horn Dust

(PURITY)

Embrace optimism, take bold actions, and trust that your desired prize is attainable.

AFFIRMATION

My heart is pure, my intentions are clear,
and I can achieve all I desire.

The unicorn has raised its head and stopped you in your tracks. That prize you are coveting or the thing you desire most is within your reach. You just need to trust that it is within your grasp and work steadily towards your goal. When you approach something with integrity and do your best, others will see this within you, and you will find you are rewarded. It could be a promotion at work or a blossoming new friendship. It may have taken time to get to where you want to be but you know you have approached your goals in the best way possible and worked hard to get what you deserve.

You may find you have to take a stab in the dark to grab hold of what is coming your way while you can. When you do, be assured that this is the right path for you and all your hard work will pay off. You will feel content and self-assured. You will raise your head up in glory and with pride just like that unicorn who is pure of spirit.

If life has been a little more difficult lately, then your unicorn may just cancel out some of the bad. But you will have to take on life with some optimism to shake off that negativity. When you are stuck in a period of doom and gloom, this can spiral into negative thought patterns, which make everything in life seem worse. In actual fact, we are always dealing with life's ups and downs — it is how we approach them that matters.

Try focussing on something positive from each day rather than dwelling on the negative. To acknowledge this, write something positive that has happened in your journal or diary each day. You may be surprised how your outlook changes, thus making your days better and brighter. When you are positive and happy this can lead to better opportunities, good experiences, and a happier future. Trust in your unicorn!

A unicorn enters the forest, making its way to a small spring to revive itself. A kaleidoscope of butterflies flutter around the unicorn, resting on its horn and flowing mane. The forest comes alive in the unicorn's presence, revering the majestic beast and blessing its journey. As it passes through; flowers bloom more brightly, and wilting plants revive. Animals come out of hiding and run alongside the great creature. They can sense the being's pure spirit and run with it unabashed and without fear. Revelling in a zest for life they hadn't felt a few minutes before. The forest loses its gloom briefly and the Sun's rays shine down on the unicorn's glorious kingdom. This essence and power comes from the unicorn's horn and must be given up voluntarily to be bottled in its most potent form. Never break a unicorn's spirit; the world could quite simply stop.

Valerian

(EARTH)

Look within to discover your inner strength, finding readiness to face any challenge.

AFFIRMATION

I am strong, powerful, and aware of my mind, body, and spirit. I have found my calm.

You have immense strength and power within, you only have to realise it. Sit calmly and look inside yourself. Now bring your attention to your centre, your core. Be aware of your breath, and realise this is where you hold your power. Focus on your breathing. If you are breathing faster than normal and taking shorter breaths, you may feel anxious. Slow your breathing. Breathe deeply right down into your belly, and find your inner strength. When you feel centred like this, you instantly feel calmer and ready to take on anything that comes your way. There is power in your breath; know you can take whatever life throws at you, whether good or bad.

Anxiety and stress may be impacting your sleep and making you feel less than tip-top. You might have a lot of nervous energy and be feeling on edge or prone to panic or anxiety attacks. To make you feel more sedate and relaxed, look inside yourself. Calm your mind, body, and spirit, and you will find your strength as you breathe deeply.

A wise old woman sits in her herb garden steeping valerian in a cauldron over a fire. She watches as the concoction boils and bubbles, finding her own form of meditation as she stares thoughtfully into the rising steam. The potion is ready and she will add it to her store to aid her customers in strength and awareness.

WOLFSBANE

(SILVER/ANTIMONY)

Embrace independence, shift old patterns, and adapt to lead a harmonious life within your pack.

AFFIRMATION

I am a shapeshifter who can adapt to any environment or situation to find my way forward.

Be ready for a new journey on an unexplored path. Don't wait for others to do things for you, it may not lead where you ultimately desire. Be a trailblazer or trendsetter. You have it within you to shift old patterns and break away from the herd. Adapt and guide your way independently through the darkness and into the light. Perhaps there is a trip you really want to take, or a project you really want to get your teeth into, but have been waiting for a friend or colleague to go with you or help you get started. Are you able to adapt your plans and go it alone? It might be just what you need and make you realise you are more than capable of doing something by or for yourself. You don't always need to wait around for someone else to be on the same page as you. You can turn the next page all by yourself simply by shifting your mindset and realising just how capable you really are. Recite the following words as a mantra:

I am courageous and independent. This is my life and I have the ability to fulfil my wildest dreams.

It might just give you a newfound confidence and release your inner (badass) wolf.

You may be an independent spirit, but this doesn't mean you shouldn't play nicely with others and become one of the pack. Don't fight against friends — they are not foes; they are there to support you. You might even be a born leader, more than capable of being a guide or role model to others. Imagine a life where you have adapted and are now living in harmony with your pack. How peaceful and nurturing does it feel? Isn't it so much better than a life where you feel like you are battling others in a constant state of fight or flight? Embrace this ability to adapt as needed, and you can choose when to run with your pack, and when to stare at the Moon in your own space.

A lone wolf howls at the Moon. The wolf is brave and free-spirited but their pack howls back in camaraderie. The wolf may journey alone, but their pack is loyal and true. The spirit of the wolf and the ability to shapeshift are captured in this luminous potion.

Wormwood

Release negativity, let go of grudges, and open the door to positive change and new opportunities in your life.

AFFIRMATION

I let go of past judgements, bitterness, and regret. I live with forgiveness to move forward in my life.

Don't let troubled times get you down or lead you down a road of bitterness or regret. Letting go of the old and any negativity you harbour will allow new positive things to enter your life. Write down what is troubling you on a scrap of paper. Acknowledge it. Then let it go. Burn or rip up the paper if you feel the need, it'll release the negativity you have been holding onto. It might also be time to rekindle an old friendship or try something different to give you a boost and let positivity back into your life.

You may feel judged or harbour resentment towards someone who has wronged you. Remember, you never know what another person is going through at a given time, they could also be feeling troubled and taking it out on you. Letting these things fester or getting angry over it won't help you in the long run. Instead, let it go. You don't need to fall out with someone, nor do you need to remain friends. Forgive this person and quietly move on if you have to. You can forge a new path and make new friendships along the way. Your heart will feel lighter, your shoulders and spirit lifted when you let go of negative thought patterns. Ultimately bringing more light, laughter, and potential opportunities into your life.

A bottle of wormwood nestles on a shelf brimming with an eclectic array of herbs and potions. Dried herbs hang haphazardly from every available surface and an earthy-smelling concoction bubbles enthusiastically in a nearby cauldron. The hedge witch reaches for the bottle of wormwood to add to her incense, banishing bad feelings and negativity from her workroom.

About the Creator

Zoe Sadler is an inky alchemist, creative seer, and illustrator.

For as long as she can remember, Zoe has loved all things mystical and magical. Inspired to transform the everyday into something extraordinary and fantastical, Zoe is an illustrator who uses ink, acrylic, and watercolour mediums to create her artwork. She is inspired by fairy tales, fantasy, and the natural world.

Zoe was brought up on a traditional croft in northern Scotland, but now lives on a small island on the southern coast of England, where she works from her studio by the sea. You can find Zoe's work in children's books, on jigsaw puzzles, and as colouring pages.

When not illustrating, Zoe can be found wandering her little island, foraging for materials to make her own ink and paint. She also enjoys wild swimming, walking her dog, and driving her vintage yellow Volkswagen Beetle. And if it's just too cold outside, you'll find her reading a good fantasy novel by the fire, with the dog curled up by her feet.

www.zoesadler.com

More from Blue Angel Publishing®

GOLDEN KEYS OF GAIA

ORACLE OF ELEMENTAL WISDOM

Vanessa Tait
Artwork by Hannah Adamaszek

Unlock the wisdom of the *Golden Keys of Gaia*, an oracle for a profound connection with Mother Earth. Drawing from Indigenous ecology, earth-based spirituality, and Tibetan wisdom, it guides inner harmony and vision manifestation.

This deck is a voice of our ancestors, reminding us of our sacred partnership with Earth. The oracle illuminates paths to discovering the Golden Keys, fostering a deeper connection with yourself, nature, and the world soul. Explore teachings that have stood the test of time, guiding you to meet the world as our ancestors once did.

May it open your heart and mind more to meet with closer connectedness to yourself, with nature and the anima mundi — the world soul. Embrace this oracle for personal growth, spiritual insight, and rekindling your profound connection with Gaia, our Great Mother Earth.

ISBN: 978-1-922574-01-5
50 cards & 208-page full-colour guidebook.

More from Blue Angel Publishing®

NOVA WITCH TAROT

WEAVE YOUR UNIQUE MAGIC INTO LIFE'S TAPESTRY

Suki Ferguson
Artwork by Ana Novaes

Do you experience life deeply, in all its light and shade? Do you long for a richer understanding of the world and your place in it?

Nova Witch Tarot is a captivating deck tailored for young hearts and those new to tarot. These 78 cards and full-colour guidebook are your trusted allies, helping you dance through life's twists and turns with empathy and self-love. Illuminate the countless facets of your being while discovering hidden potential and unexpected paths into the future.

ISBN: 978-1-922574-05-3
78 cards & 112-page full-colour guidebook.

More from Blue Angel Publishing®

MOON TEMPLE ORACLE

YOUR PERSONAL PORTAL TO THE COSMOS

Suzy Cherub
Artwork by Laila Savolainen

Welcome to the enchanting realm of the *Moon Temple Oracle*. Immerse yourself in the potent cycle of the moon, exploring the vast tapestry of magic and divine lunar influences worldwide. This deck is your companion and conduit to attune to lunar energies and integrate celestial guidance into your daily life.

Unlock the secrets of 11 moon temples and their guardians, unveiling profound messages for navigating our ever-evolving existence. Ancient wisdom seamlessly intertwines with contemporary spirituality, ensuring the relevance and depth of each message. Let the exquisite artwork transport you as you embody the archetypes within each card through sacred rituals and practices. Weave the wisdom of lunar deities like Abuk, Mayari, Phoebe and others into your human journey.

Enter the *Moon Temple Oracle* – a cosmic invitation to discover, connect and thrive.

ISBN: 978-1-922574-22-0
44 cards & 256-page full-colour guidebook.

More from Blue Angel Publishing®

ANIMAL GUIDE RUNE CARDS

Dawid Lipka and Bartosz Mazik

Embark on a magical journey as you unlock the wisdom of nature and ancient Norse runes with the *Animal Guide Rune Cards*. This captivating deck weaves together the potent symbolism of foxdeers and owls, bats and badgers, merging the power of the animal kingdom with the esoteric mysteries of runic lore.

Discover the profound and practical insights offered by each of the 25 strikingly illustrated cards and accompanying messages, illuminating every aspect of your life, from relationships to health to career choices. The comprehensive guidebook also includes instructions for creating spellbinding runic talismans and reveals the connections between the runes and tarot, astrology and the chakras. Immerse yourself in the wisdom of the runes and delve into the mythic and cultural philosophy they embody.

Divine your destiny by journeying into the enchanting realm of the Elder Futhark, allowing your animal guides to lead you every step of the way.

ISBN: 978-1-922574-06-0
25 cards & 288-page full-colour guidebook.

For more information on this or
any Blue Angel Publishing release,
please visit our website at:

WWW.BLUEANGELONLINE.COM